Most Valuable Player

Hakeem Olajuwon

Chris W. Sehnert

Published by Abdo & Daughters, 4940 Viking Drive, Suite 622, Edina, Minnesota 55435.

Copyright © 1996 by Abdo Consulting Group, Inc., Pentagon Tower, P.O. Box 36036, Minneapolis, Minnesota 55435 USA. International copyrights reserved in all countries. No part of this book may be reproduced in any form without written permission from the publisher.

Printed in the United States.

Cover Photo credit: Allsport Photos
Interior Photo credits: Wide World Photos, pages 5, 14, 21, 24, 27, 29
                              Bettmann Photos, page 11

Edited by Paul Joseph

Library of Congress Cataloging-in-Publication Data

Sehnert, Chris W.
        Hakeem Olajuwon /Chris W. Sehnert
        p. cm. -- (MVP)
        Includes index
Summary: Profiles the career of the Nigerian born basketball player who brought the Houston Rockets it's first NBA Title and who achieved the MVP award for himself.
ISBN 1-56239-542-4
1. Olajuwon, Hakeem, 1963- --Juvenile literature. 2. Basketball players--United States--Biography--Juvenile literature. 3. Houston Rockets (Basketball team) --Juvenile literature. [1. Olajuwon, Hakeem, 1963- . 2. Basketball players. 3. Blacks-Nigeria-Biography.] I. Title. II Series: M.V.P.. most valuable player.
GV884.O43S45 1996
786.323'092--dc20
[B]   95-45629
                                                                CIP
                                                                 AC

Contents

HAKEEM THE DREAM

A seven-foot monster looms in the lane. He is a giant among giants in the National Basketball Association (NBA). He can dunk the ball through the hoop with ferocious power. He can shoot the turnaround jumper with the grace of a guard. On defense, he protects the basket—swatting shots out of midair, and wrestling rebounds off the glass.

Hakeem Olajuwon is a nightmare to his opponents. His fans call him "The Dream." The Houston Rockets have won two straight NBA titles with Hakeem leading the way. He has come from an island in Africa to become the NBA's Most Valuable Player.

Hakeem Olajuwon fights for a rebound.

HAKEEM'S HOMETOWN

Hakeem Abdul Ajibola Olajuwon was born January 21, 1963, in Lagos, Nigeria. Lagos is a crowded island town located in the Gulf of Guinea. It's connected to the continent of Africa by bridges.

Lagos is a merchant town. People fill the streets buying and selling the goods that ships bring into the harbor. Cows, chickens, goats and other livestock roam the streets as well.

Hakeem's family descended from the Yoruban culture. They are Islamic, which means their religion is Moslem. Hakeem's father, Salaam, and mother, Abike, owned a concrete business in Lagos. (Many of the houses there are made of cement.)

Hakeem has four brothers and one sister. They grew up together in a one-story, three-bedroom house. The Olajuwon's tried to live by three family rules: study hard in school, keep away from bad people, and always stay calm and collected.

Hakeem grew very tall at a young age. Sometimes, he felt bad about being different. The neighborhood kids would tease him. He didn't always follow his family's rules. He would get into fights when he was teased too much.

A simple dirt field with a soccer goal on one end was the only playground in town. This is where Hakeem found his love for sports.

Soccer and team handball were the popular sports in Lagos. Team handball is a field sport much like soccer, where the use of hands is allowed. Hakeem's size and athletic ability made him an excellent player. He liked to play goalie when he played soccer.

WHAT IS BASKETBALL?

Hakeem was 6 feet, 9 inches tall when he was 15 years old. He attended the Moslem Teachers College, which is where teenagers in Lagos go instead of high school. While at this school, Hakeem learned to speak English. He also became acquainted with the game of basketball.

The coach of the Lagos State basketball team was a man named Ganiyu Otenigbade. One day late in 1978, he was walking past the playground in Lagos. He spotted Hakeem leaning up against the soccer goal. He asked Hakeem if he would like to play basketball.

Hakeem had never even seen a basketball game. But judging from his great size, the coach knew he could become a great player.

He convinced Hakeem to split his time between team handball and this new sport.

In 1979, Hakeem began playing basketball for the Lagos State junior team. His coach was Sunday Osagiede, nicknamed Sunny Basket. Sunny was a point guard for the Nigerian national team.

"Back then Hakeem was more famous for handball," Sunny said. "In the national all-sports festival I had an ambulance waiting to rush Hakeem from his handball games to our basketball games so he could help us two ways." Hakeem ended up being the leading scorer in handball. And in basketball, he was the leader in both scoring and rebounding. Lagos State won gold medals in both.

NIGERIAN NATIONAL TEAM

Hakeem continued to grow. At the age of 17, he was 6 feet, 11 inches tall. Basketball became his primary sport of interest. He played in the Lagos club league, and then joined Nigeria's junior national team.

Hakeem was still very inexperienced on the basketball floor. His new coach, Richard Mills, taught him many skills. He wanted Hakeem to use his size and be more aggressive.

He was the first coach to put Hakeem at the center position, and the person who showed Hakeem how to dunk!

The 1980 All African Games were held in Casablanca, Morocco. With the support of coach Mills, Hakeem was asked to play for the Nigerian national team. He had played basketball for less than two years, and had already reached Africa's highest level of competition.

COMING TO AMERICA

Education was very important to the Olajuwon family. Hakeem's oldest brother, Kaka, studied in London, England. His sister, Kudi, went to college in Cairo, Egypt. Hakeem wanted to leave home for college, too.

The Nigerian national basketball team gave Hakeem the chance to travel and play all around Africa. This gave more people a chance to see Hakeem play. One person who took notice was a United States State Department employee named Chris Pond.

Pond met Hakeem while coaching basketball in an international club tournament. He knew that a player of Hakeem's size and intelligence would be welcome at an American University. Hakeem listened, and Pond made arrangements for him to visit several college campuses in the United States.

UNIVERSITY OF HOUSTON

In October of 1980, Hakeem came to America. His first stop was New York City. He was not accustomed to the northern climate, and did not like being cold. He was told it was warm in Texas, so he traveled to Houston.

Guy Lewis was the basketball coach at the University of Houston. He was immediately impressed with Hakeem's height. After watching him practice, however, Lewis knew Hakeem would need to learn the American style of basketball. He also wanted Hakeem to go into training and build his muscles.

Hakeem decided to stay in Houston. He wanted to start playing for the Cougars right away. He would not begin practicing with the team until after the 1980-81 season. Following coach Lewis' instructions, Hakeem spent the year preparing himself in the fundamentals of American college basketball.

Opposite page:
University of Houston's Hakeem
Olajuwon gets ready to slam
dunk against Rice, 1984.

STRANGE LAND

Hakeem's first year in America was a learning experience. He was not used to the customs of his new country. Everything from the food to the clothing was foreign to him. The customs he carried from Nigeria included bowing to people upon greeting them, wearing traditional African clothes, and eating rice, which was the only food he could find that reminded him of home.

Hakeem's new friends helped to "Americanize" him. Soon he was wearing designer clothes, and dancing at local clubs. Gaining weight for the team was no longer a problem either. His new favorite foods were T-bone steaks and ice cream. He went from a thin, 190 pounds (86 kg) to a husky, 245 pounds (111 kg) in one year.

Calling home twice-a-week kept Hakeem from getting lonely. His parents were more interested in his schooling than his basketball career. Hakeem was excellent in school, where he studied business technology.

Hakeem sat directly behind the bench for each University of Houston home game. He loved the excitement of the American college game. With every dunk he would stand and scream. He could hardly wait for his turn on the floor.

FRESHMAN WOES

Hakeem's freshman season came in 1981-82. The Cougars were a solid team led by Houston native, Clyde "The Glide" Drexler. They advanced to the NCAA (National Collegiate Athletic Association) tournament's Final Four. The North Carolina Tar Heels, led by Michael Jordan, knocked off Houston in the semi-final round on their way to becoming NCAA champions.

Hakeem was not quite ready for the type of game Houston played. The Cougars were a running team. Their offensive attack depended on players who could get up and down the floor swiftly. When Hakeem played, he would get into foul trouble early and often. He could not keep up with the fast pace.

Coach Lewis was tough on Hakeem. When he was taken out of games, Hakeem would become angry with his coach. He didn't understand that the coach was pushing him to work harder. Lewis knew Hakeem had tremendous potential, but he needed to improve his game.

MOSES GUIDES HAKEEM

After the season, Hakeem found the perfect practice companion. Moses Malone, a star NBA center, was living in the Houston area. He had seen Hakeem play for the Cougars, and asked him to a game of one-on-one.

Two founding members of Phi Slama Jama:
Clyde Drexler (left) and Hakeem Olajuwon.

Moses and Hakeem became good friends. Soon, they were practicing together every day. Their one-on-one challenges became a battle of the big men. Each would learn from the other. Both improved their game as a result. It was just the workout Hakeem needed to get ready for his sophomore season.

PHI SLAMA JAMA

A new fraternity was formed on the University of Houston campus during the 1982-83 season. It was the high-flying, shot-blocking, slam-dunking Houston Cougars. They became known as the "House of Phi Slama Jama." Basketball fans everywhere gathered to watch their weekly meetings.

Those who watched were rarely disappointed. The Cougars piled up 25 straight wins on their way to a 31-3 record. By the end of the regular season, they were ranked as the best team in the nation.

At 20 years old, Hakeem had come of age. He led all college basketball players with 175 blocked shots. He averaged more than 13 points per game, and had 68 slam dunks!

Hakeem's fraternity brothers included Clyde Drexler, Larry Micheaux, Benny Anders and Michael Young. Together, they advanced to the NCAA's Final Four for the second year in a row.

In the semifinal matchup, the Cougars met the Louisville Cardinals. Hakeem dominated. He scored 21 points, pulled down 22 rebounds, and blocked 8 shots. Houston won the game 94-81. They would meet Cinderella in the NCAA final.

The North Carolina State Wolfpack lost 10 regular season games in 1982-83, but they were a team of destiny. They defeated the heavily favored Cougars 54-52 to win the NCAA Basketball Championship.

Hakeem played an excellent game. He scored 20 points, had 18 rebounds and blocked 11 shots. Everything else the Cougars did seemed to go wrong.

The score was tied 52-52 with just seconds remaining on the game clock. North Carolina State's Dereck Whittenburg threw up a long jump shot, and Hakeem prepared himself for the rebound. It never came. The shot was an air ball. The Wolfpack's Lorenzo Charles caught it on the way down, and slammed it home as the buzzer sounded.

Hakeem was voted the tournament's Most Valuable Player. It was the first time in 17 years a player from a non-winning team had won the award. Hakeem would have rather won the championship trophy for his team.

OLAJUWON VS. EWING

Six members of Phi Slama Jama graduated after the 1982-83 season. Among the graduates was Clyde "The Glide" Drexler, who moved on to the NBA. Hakeem stayed, and the Cougars rode him back to the Final Four.

Hakeem had become a household word after his performance in the 1983 NCAA Tournament. He was known as one of the two best centers in college basketball. The other was the Georgetown Hoyas' Patrick Ewing.

After another outstanding season with the Cougars, Hakeem would meet Ewing in the 1984 NCAA final. Hakeem had more rebounds than any college player during the 1983-84 season. And he had the highest shooting accuracy at 67.5 percent.

The showdown in the 1984 championship game would be the first of many for the two future NBA stars. Unfortunately for Hakeem, he lost round one. The Hoyas prevailed 84-75. Hakeem and the Cougars had been to the NCAA Final Four three straight years without a championship.

ROCKET MAN

Hakeem left the University of Houston after his junior season. He stayed in town, however. The NBA's Houston Rockets had the first pick in the 1984 draft. They chose Hakeem ahead of a long list of candidates including Michael Jordan, Charles Barkley, Sam Perkins and John Stockton.

At seven-feet tall, Hakeem would not be the tallest member of his new team. The Rockets already had Ralph Sampson, the NBA's 1983-84 rookie-of the-year. Sampson was seven-feet, four-inches tall. The two became known as Houston's "Twin Towers."

Hakeem established himself as a force in the NBA from the beginning. The Rockets won only 29 of 82 games the year before his arrival. In Hakeem's rookie season, the Rockets headed to the playoffs with a second-place finish in the Midwest Division.

Hakeem averaged 20.6 points and 11.9 rebounds per game in his first professional season. He was among the league leaders in blocked shots. He finished second in the rookie-of-the-year voting, behind Michael Jordan.

HAKEEM REACHES THE FINALS

The 1985-86 season was Hakeem's second in the NBA.
He placed second in the All-Star balloting behind Los
Angeles Lakers center Kareem Abdul-Jabbar. The
Rockets were the Western Conference Champions.
They met the Boston Celtics in the NBA Finals.

Hakeem improved his scoring average to 23.5 points per
game in 1985-86. He finished among the league leaders
in rebounds and blocked shots. At 23 years old, he was
regarded as one of the games' finest players.

The Rockets faced the defending NBA champion Lakers
in the conference finals. Hakeem averaged 30 points,
12 rebounds and 4 blocked shots per game in the best-
of-seven series. He out-dueled the veteran Abdul-
Jabbar to lead the Rockets to victory in five games.

The Rockets had risen from the basement of the
standings to reach the NBA Finals in just two seasons.
Their opponents, the Boston Celtics, were a perennial
powerhouse.

The Celtics countered Houston's "Twin Towers" with
veterans Bill Walton, Robert Parish and Kevin McHale
on the inside. Larry Bird, the league's MVP that year,
was unstoppable from the outside.

The Celtics' balanced attack and veteran leadership prevailed. They defeated the Rockets in six games to become the 1986 NBA champions. Hakeem's performance in the series was excellent. Just as in college, however, his team was the runner-up.

BROKEN DREAM

The Rockets' rise to the top of the NBA went suddenly off-course after the 1985-86 season. Hakeem remained a constant force, while the rest of the organization struggled. For the next seven seasons, the Rockets tried new players, new coaches, and finally new ownership.

Hakeem was becoming known as the best player never to win a championship. He made the NBA All-Star team every year, but his team never made it past the early rounds of the playoffs. In the 1988-89 season, Hakeem became the first player to have more than 200 steals (213) and 200 blocked shots (282) in a season. He won the NBA's rebounding title in 1989, and in 1990 he led the league in rebounds and blocked shots.

Hakeem was performing in his usual way on January 3, 1991, when an accidental elbow nearly ended his career. It came from Bill Cartwright, the Chicago Bulls center,

Hakeem drives to the basket as Phoenix Suns Kevin Johnson (7) falls backwards.

and shattered the bone structure around Hakeem's right eye. The result of the injury turned out to be a wake-up call for the rest of the Rockets. While Hakeem was sidelined, the remaining players came together as a team. They won 15 of the 25 games he sat out.

When Hakeem returned, the Rockets were even better, winning 13 games in a row. Despite his injury, Hakeem led the league in blocked shots for the second straight season. The Los Angeles Lakers knocked them out of the playoffs in the first round, however.

The Rockets' inability to win a championship was hard for Hakeem to take. He complained to management often concerning their commitment to winning. In the 1991-92 season, the Rockets failed to make the playoffs for the first time in Hakeem's career. When the season was over he asked to be traded.

DON'T TRADE THE FRANCHISE!

Rudy Tomjanovich took over as head coach of the Rockets for the 1992-93 season. He brought with him a new offensive plan which focused on Hakeem's ability to score. Tomjanovich requested that management not trade their star player. Hakeem stayed and posted the best season of his career.

The Rockets went 55-27 to win their first division title since 1986. Hakeem led the league in blocked shots for the third year in a row. He became only the third NBA player in history to record 2000 points, 1000 rebounds, and 300 blocked shots in a season.

Hakeem was named the NBA's defensive player-of-the-year. He finished second in the voting for MVP behind Charles Barkley of the Phoenix Suns. The Rockets lost to the Seattle Supersonics in the second round of the playoffs. It was clear, however, that a new era had begun in Houston.

BLAST-OFF!

The Rockets began the 1993-94 season with 15 straight victories. They ended it as champions of the NBA! Hakeem's long-awaited dream had come true.

Houston went 58-24 to capture their second-straight division title. Hakeem averaged 27.3 points per game. He was named the defensive player-of-the-year for the second time in a row. His 3.5 assists per game was a career best. Hakeem Olajuwon was named the Most Valuable Player in the NBA.

This time the Rockets would not be grounded in the playoffs. They defeated the Portland Trail Blazers, Phoenix Suns, and Utah Jazz on their way to the NBA Finals.

Hakeem (34) dunks the ball over New York Knicks center Patrick Ewing, (right).

Their opponents in the championship series were the New York Knicks.

Starring for the Knicks was Patrick Ewing. It was a rematch of the centers from the 1984 NCAA final. The championship would be decided in seven games. When it was over, the Rockets had brought Houston their first title in a major sporting event.

Hakeem averaged 27 points and 10 rebounds per game in the final series. He was named MVP of the finals. His shot block in the closing seconds of game six was a game saver. He would forever be remembered as a champion.

REPEAT

After waiting 10 years for his first NBA title, Hakeem didn't waste time getting number two. The Rockets were NBA champions again in 1995. This time an old teammate was there to share the glory.

Clyde Drexler was traded to the Rockets in mid-season. He joined his old "Phi Slama Jama" brother for a historic playoff run. The Rockets needed to defeat the top three teams in the conference to reach the finals. They finished off the Utah Jazz and the Phoenix Suns before beating the San Antonio Spurs in the conference championship.

The Rockets faced the Orlando Magic in the NBA Finals. Hakeem was unstoppable. He was 32 years old and playing better than ever. He averaged 33 points and 10.3 rebounds per game while facing Shaquille O'Neal, the Magic's young star.

Houston won four straight games to sweep the finals and bring home their second NBA Championship in as many years. Hakeem was named the MVP of the championship series for the second year in a row. His place in the NBA history books was secure.

BEING ON TOP

Hakeem is a humble and devoutly religious man. His generosity and charitable work go largely unnoticed because he does not like to bring attention to himself. When he was awarded with the NBA's MVP trophy, he invited all of his teammates onto the floor to accept it with him.

In April 1993, Hakeem became a citizen of the United States. He has never forgotten his early days in Africa, however. He is the official spokesperson for NBA International, which promotes basketball around the globe. He also has his own company which seeks business opportunities worldwide.

Reunited "Phi Slama Jama" brothers, Hakeem (left) and Drexler (center), celebrate with teammate Charles Jones minutes before they won the NBA championship.

Hakeem lives outside of Houston in a house which he helped design. The architecture is a larger version of the villa in Lagos where he grew up.

The name Olajuwon means *being on top*, and Hakeem has done much to live up to it. He has worked consistently to improve his game since the first time he picked up a basketball at the age of 15. He is now considered among the greatest to have ever played the game of basketball.

HAKEEM OLAJUWON'S ADDRESS

You can write to Hakeem Olajuwon at the following address:

Hakeem Olajuwon
c/o Houston Rockets
The Summit
10 Greenway Plaza
East Houston, TX 77046

If you want a response, please enclose a self-addressed, stamped envelope.

Hakeem's dream.

GLOSSARY

All-Star: A player who is voted by fans as the best player at his position that year.

Assist: A pass of a basketball that enables a teammate to score.

Cinderella: A team which wins unexpectedly.

Dunk: To slam a ball through the basket from above.

Final Four: The name given to the last four teams remaining in the NCAA college basketball championship tournament.

Foul: Illegal contact with another player. Basketball players are allowed a limited amount of fouls per game, usually five or six.

Foul Out: To be put out of a game for exceeding the number of permissible fouls.

Fraternity: An organization of male students at a college or university, usually designated by Greek letters.

Goalie: A player assigned to protect the goal in various sports.

Gulf of Guinea: A body of water located off the western coast of Africa.

Merchant: One whose occupation is the wholesale purchase and retail sale of goods for profit.

Moslem: A religion characterized by the acceptance of Mohammed as the chief and last prophet of God.

NBA (National Basketball Association): The professional basketball league in North America.

NCAA (National Collegiate Athletic Association): An organization which oversees the administration of college athletics.

Nigeria: A country in Northwest Africa.

Rebound: To retrieve and gain possession of the ball as it bounces off the backboard or rim after an unsuccessful shot.

United States State Department: A division of the government involved in international relations.

Yoruba: West-African people living chiefly in Southwest Nigeria.

Index